dreaming with my eyes open

michela perry

ISBN: 978-1-966798-38-5

Cover by: Rein G

Illustrations by: Rein G and Méyara Black

Edited by: W K Waite-Gracie

Whether it is the best of times or the worst of times, it is the only time we have.

—Art Buchwald

Tamey, mum and nana, this one's for you.

the tide is changing
i feel it in my bones
are you alive today
or are you just living
feeling lost

as the leaves fall to the ground
i shed memories
layers
reminding me that tomorrow is not
promised
our leaves could turn at any time
fall at any moment
any season could be mine

fallen

CHANGES

i know today was hard
a change in seasons
in your life
and with Mother Earth

i promise that it always gets better you are
not alone
you are more than what you think

you are worthy
of everything this life has to offer

i'm here with you - michela perry

TWIN FLAME

the sun and the moon
are everything
i aspire to be
as bright as they are
they have balance
rotate in translation
they understand each other replicating soul
mates,
twin flames

find your balance

breathing in **8 Acres Coffee** as the fresh air
reminds me how grateful i am to be here
to be alive
to be breathing
in this very moment
keeping me grounded
taking a quick glance behind to see how far
i've come
because after you read this
everything changes

manifest

throw on your favourite baggy hoodie grab
a blanket
and take a few moments for yourself you
deserve this

choose yourself

YOU ARE LOVED

every night before bed
have a look up at the sky
look at the stars
and realize how small we are
we take so much for granted and complain
about everything when all we really want to
be is a star

shining in the darkest of rooms even if it's
our own
speaking
even when our voices are not heard

just know
i hear you
i see you,
star

thank you for being a light

i keep waiting for change
nothing is happening

make the first move

WOMEN KNOW CHANGE

change in our bodies
our lifestyle
our face
our, flower

our bodies are ever changing while we
adapt
adapt to our hormones
periods
partners
kids
love

when we step outside
we look around
for change
a change in movement
vehicles
sometimes find change in our own shadows

we change constantly
yet we fear change
change of the unknown

change of appearances
change of love
change of heart

change on your own terms

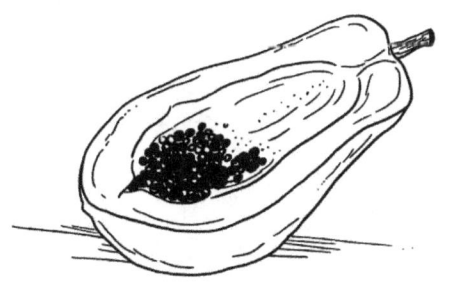

don't underestimate yourself today
you're beautiful

you got this

WODA CODA

the wind changes in the direction
in which my love follows you
and the light reminds me
of every good memory I have experienced
with you

you are my light
please don't ever stop being that
i will always follow you home

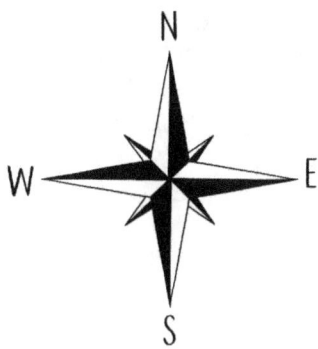

If you're here right now, reading this
i want you to know that i'm proud of you
and that you're loved

you're doing great, keep trying
i'm rooting for you.

growing pains - michela perry

GROW FLOWERS OVER YOUR WOUNDS

i feel like i'm addicted to writing, addicted to feeling, expressing. i have never been like this before. i was never shown how to express myself, only in acts of anger, yelling, destruction, fighting, don't show weakness, don't cry. but now, i feel like i am able to share my writings with you because i've learned how to grow, heal, and accept all the good things into my life, while deleting the rest.

learning how to grow flowers over your pain is hard.
learning to look into the mirror and tell yourself you're beautiful is hard.
learning to accept yourself for who you are, without the approval of anyone else, is hard. but it's worth it. if you're not where you want to be in your life, keep going. i see your potential, you see your potential. i

don't care what anyone else has said to you
before, i'm glad you're here. sink your bare
feet slowly down into Mother Earth, let her
work through you.

YOU ARE NOT DEFINED
BY YOUR PAST

JUST BREATHE

every morning i close my eyes,
tilt my head slightly back
take a breath
and remind myself how thankful i am

TICKING

how many days
am i able to look in the mirror
in constant routine
of brushing my hair
like a live time lapse
right before my eyes
as i watch myself
change
age
look more like my parents,
my nana,
grow
heal

one day i'll look into the mirror
and it'll be my last glance
at my perfect imperfections
my curls
my eyes
my life.

be kind to your tethered soul
(stay golden)

MISS YOU MUM

my heart has never felt an ache
so deep
penetrating my nerves to get under them an
ache so heavy
that it hurts to breathe
to think
about anything else
coming to the realization
that i have to live this life without you
an absence in my reality
unknown change
that i'm not okay with.

note:
3 months in isolation after my mum's passing, i learned
how to think and fend for myself, in the middle of
nowhere ish (wandering river, alberta, canada)
our friends joanne and gord welcomed us into their home
during this time, i can never say thank you enough. for
providing a safe space and time to heal, to cry really really
loud and to feel. I lost my step mum Tamey and then I
lost my mum. a double blow to the chest. If you've ever
lost a parent or someone very close to you, just know

healing will be the best thing for you. i know it's hard and
it f*cking hurts, but keep going. it gets better, i swear.

i've been missing you a lot lately
i always wonder when you're peeking
down through heaven's long white curtains
to check in on us making sure we're okay.

TIME FOR MYSELF

today is for me
breathing in nature
holding it in my diaphragm
exhaling all the negative out
what my body doesn't need
i am beautiful
i love who i am
i love my life
x repeat

i know what i need today
s p a c e
i'll rejoin the world when i'm ready

- brb

PACE YOURSELF

i'm taking time to heal and that's okay.

waking up while the sun lights up the room
watching the branches dance in the wind
showing me their shadows through the
blinds, their true self.

(today's going to be a good day)

EVICTION

i stopped cooking for myself
when i didn't need it as a survival skill
anymore

wander,
then come back to yourself.

looking back at old photos of strangers,
people who have lived before us
stood in the same spot, before us
standing in memories
while making new ones
souls that have left this earth
replaced by new faces

nostalgic,
wanting to time travel
back to these very moments
someone's 'happy'
someone's 'sad'

someone's funeral

my path has brought me here
stepping into your memory
your existence
and out of my reality
to be here, present
in the wind
with you.
i wish i didn't overthink every decision,
every moment. confirmation for something i
already know. or something i don't. since i
was young i was like this. asking permission
to go in our fridge. asking to have a snack, a
drink. asking to wear a certain sweater to
step outside. i used to think this was me
being polite, shy even. i think my brain is
wired differently. i often feel like this, feel
like i hide it. hide my extremely quick
detailed thoughts, suppress them. is there
something wrong with the way my

thoughts are organized? i know i'm
different, as we all are. but sometimes,
i feel like i'm missing something.

my heart starts to race
before i speak
but i know
I'll kill it anyways

believe in your skills

when someone underestimates you,
remember that you're a rockstar.

REFLECT

my soul rejuvenates
as the colours change
breathing in every ounce of the morning
brisk
and the way the waves in your hair reflect
on all the light
the sun has to give

deep breath

the beginning of love
at any age,
is young love.

better yourself
but don't change for someone who is
temporary

THINGS WILL GET BETTER

why is the silence so loud today?

I promise you that
we will never have enough time with our
loved ones.

(my nana Saverina passed away peacefully
and suddenly this morning)

hold yourself to a standard so high
that respect is the first thing people think
when they meet you

POSITIVE VIBES

another heavy hitter loss,
losing tamey, mum, and now nana

you can never prepare for death
whether it's sudden or expected

death will always be lurking
nonbiased in its natural state
favors no one
and waits for no one

a clock that never stops ticking,
until it does

be ready
treat every last moment with someone like
it's their last

because this is number 3 for me
powerful, strong, female mother figures in
my life and i'm telling you right now

it hurts just as bad each time

love more.

get off your phone
pay attention to detail
when someone's talking to you,
listen

be ready
because when it happens
it will side swipe you at the knees,
everytime
be ready
dig into your culture
plant roots in your family
be vulnerable with them
but love more
Respect your elders
learn from them
their knowledge
their traumas

who they really are
because it's a big part of who YOU are.

be ready.

my heart rate increases
unable to see from the ocean in my eyes
losing room for air
as my chest fills with deep sadness
where do I go from here?

as i'm adapting to losing a close loved one
once again,
i'm reminded that time is infinite
but OUR time we have is miniscule

a blip in our timeline
a blink and it's gone

don't wish for more time
use the time you have now
and hold yourself accountable

because once it's gone
that's it.

i'm trying to channel my angels on heaven's radio.

dial tone

I need to dig deep into my faith, or I will lose myself.

BLINDSIDED

you were just here on monday
and you went to heaven on Wednesday

leaving behind purchased fruit, bread
and empty bottles

as i clean up
the aftermath of what's left from your last
visit
your last, last visit

i can still feel your presence
your scent still stained and lingers on this
blanket
that i'm afraid to use,
so i don't lose that last piece of your
physical footprint

to not forget what you smelt like

to not forget how much you loved our
cabin-like home
to not forget the way you would endlessly
clean
to not forget the way you would fall asleep
on the couch sitting up, with your feet
crossed to not forget the way you would say
"moo-kyla"
to not forget the way you loved us

as i clean up
the aftermath of what's left of your last visit

i'm recycling your very last Sanpellegrino
bottle you touched
so i can put flowers in it

as a daily reminder of you
and your love for this drink that I very
much did not enjoy

i will forever miss the sound of you doing
dishes way too early in the morning that i
was too grumpy to appreciate
or the way you shuffled in the house with
your flip flops, slippers
or the way you would sacrifice your comfort
for someone else to have it as i continue to
heal,

i'm reminded that you were the pinnacle of
our family
a Polynesian pioneer
and i will use your soul and light
as a guide on how to carry myself
and love one another like you did
being grateful for you is an understatement
my love for you, our relationship
stretches way beyond this earth
i'm very proud to be your granddaughter,
your namesake.
Saverina Peter's granddaughter.

thank you for this life nana.

visit me in my dreams

i'm tired of losing loved ones.

DEATH MAKES PEOPLE WEIRD

you are not obligated to check in when you feel checked out.

before i go

another piece of me is missing
like when the sun sets and takes its warmth
away from the hills

i could never thank her enough
a soul connection so deep it seeps through
my skin
and radiates through my eyes

#virgo

when my time is up
i want to be buried in the dirt
giving myself back to Mother Earth
surrounded by loved ones
hymns, and music
piano in the background
being played softly
but loud enough that it echoes the walls

behind your eyes,
as it enters through your ears
like a portal
a portal i get to float through
getting to see my ancestors again
a place in eternity i can rest
fully rest
and be at peace
right here,
i will wait for you.

are you happy?
or are you just idling.

leave me with a pumpkin spice
an oversized blanket
piano playing
scented candles
harry potter, twilight
halloween movies
with fall decorations
in every corner of my house

so that i can breathe in
every aspect of fall
and know that a new season
is upon me

everywhere my eyes gaze in this home
i find pieces of me and you intertwined
of who we are together
but i also find pieces of us individually,
and i like that.

what you would do for her
and what you would do to her
are two different things

i would travel through space and time
to see you through a parallel universe
to send you messages
to let you know
that i'm still here,
around you.

LOVE CONQUERS ALL

stare at the stars
knowing there's something else past it,
beyond us

there is where you'll find home
where you'll find yourself,
and where you'll find me.

i've experienced deep loss
and for that
i'm not afraid of death
but I am afraid of time.

gone gone, gone
how many people leave until
there's no one left.

passed souls

people will always try to claim something or
someone once they're gone
why not when they're here?
why not claim who you are, now?

I've been drowning for so long
that it almost feels like floating
wading in the water
keeping my mouth above the surface
slow breaths
to not waste energy, oxygen
until i'm able to float to shore
or until someone sees me
and can rescue me.

lifejacket

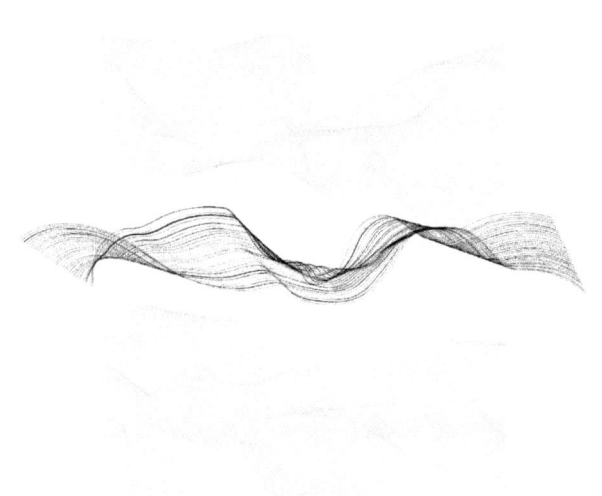

everytime a wave hits
i don't know if i should go with it
or against it

the way you swish your coffee
that's been sitting for a few mins too long
for your liking

the way you emphasize your 'U's, words
with U's
to describe you

unstoppable, unconditional, unforgettable
you're unique
the most beautiful wave
that has ever come over me
and take me under

an underwater world
that i never want to leave
or forget

i would rather run out of oxygen
then head to the surface
if that meant never seeing you again,
then i'll risk everything for that.

we are all just specks of dust in the sunlight
trying to find our way.

don't forget your roots
don't forget why you're here.

the emptiness
and lack of hope
that surrounds these white walls
is echoing

yet defining
of what we are yet to experience
of what we have seen so far
things that we can never unsee
permanent wounds
that will forever bleed,
slowly.

hospital

my mind constantly searches
through the pages
where memories of you are imprinted
folding down the corners
to always come back to my favourite parts.

when people ask when i'm fine
i am
until i think about if i am
maybe i'm not
maybe i'm pretending

my pillows have heard me cry
and caught my tears
yet i'm silent when you're in front of me

my eyes gaze out the window
up to the sky
waiting to see something
hoping for anything.

everything stands still
when you're in front of me
the wind holds time in place
while i focus on your eyes
the pain and love it has experienced in this
life
you are a wildflower
that has been intentionally planted
on my path
a path that i never want to leave.

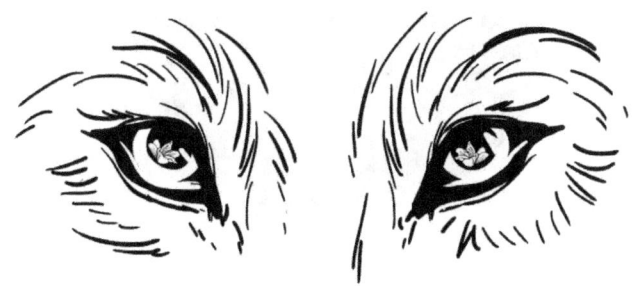

to be loved by you
is something that i never knew i needed.

hearing stories about you
from someone else's perspective
brings me unusually closer to you it helps
me remember
what your life was like before me, before i
was born.

letting go has never felt so good.

these uninvited negative thoughts i have
held firmly in my hands
and crushed to save myself
from myself.

your voice brings me back
to a calm place
when i struggle to find myself
when i feel lost in the woods.

WINTER DREAMING

staring out the window mid-winter
watching snowflakes cling to anything it
finds
while my breath fogs up my view of reality
and what I deeply wish to see instead.

i am who i am because of my sisters.

THERAPY

the bridge between us has been burned
not only to bring us closer
but to appreciate memories of what used to
be there
and where we are now,
without the gap.

standing on the edge between dreaming and
reality
but i don't know anymore which side is real
and which isn't.

some days you need to choose isolation
spend time with yourself
and heal.

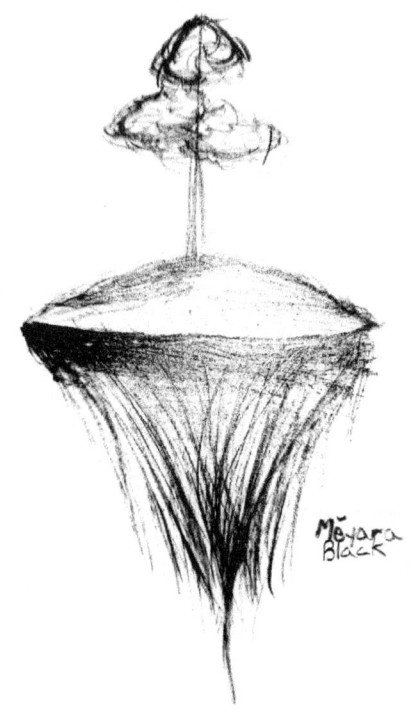

holding onto hope
even if it's by a thread.

do not waste my time. if you don't plan on investing in more time. to keep track of the time we share. do not waste my time if you don't know how to spend it.

APPRECIATE HER

8 years sober from alcohol

8 years since tamey passed

3 years since mum passed

9 months since nana passed

5 months since poppy passed.

a numbers game that doesn't stop counting.

if we were vampires,
death would be non-existent,
it would be a joke
watching humans cling onto life
wasting their time
to only regret it in the end.

BWTHHYBL

if you're looking for me
I'll be tucked in
between the cracks of the sidewalk.

OATIE

drowning underneath the ocean
that sits so heavy on my chest
a glimmer of hope found in every stranger
a part of me hopes to leave with them after
each encounter

but lost i am no more
sinking myself deep into this home
creating roots
in a place that i wish to never leave.

pine needles sticking in my bones
protecting while inflicting pain
adaptable with growth
exposed,
reaching up to the sun
because that's the direction i'll grow
that's the direction i'll glow.

a clutter in my house
means a clutter in my mind.

POV: get up

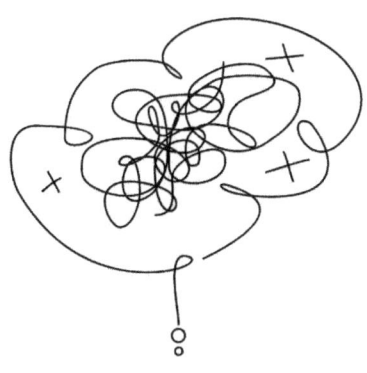

drifting away from the
one place that felt like home.

you've drifted up into the clouds
to the one place that feels like home.

my heart aches for
the future that is unknown.

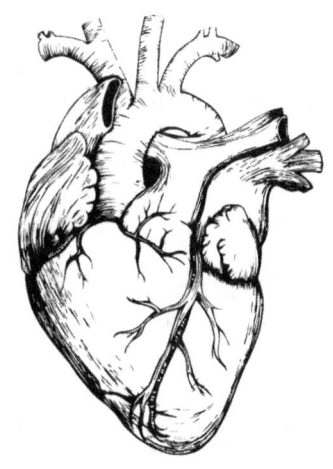

the little 'hellos'
that i get from long time strangers
familiar faces
childhood memories
that make me feel closer to you
even when your physical isn't present
i hope they continue to see you
in my mannerisms and laughs,
so that I can also see them through your
eyes.

mum and I locked eyes as she took her last
few breaths she was the first one i saw when
i entered the world
and i'm the last thing she saw when she left

funny how life works
the gift of life
breathing oxygen into our lungs
gone in a second without it

fragile thought
followed by excruciating pain
memories of that moment
but also, not many people get that bonding
experience
to witness a soul leaving
to comfort someone while they pass

gift and a curse

grief is something that is hard to explain.
trying to explain the way your chest aches.
the actual feeling of heartbreak. breaking.
that's what it feels like. breaking from the
inside out. releasing through tears. even if
you hold your chest to try and stop the pain,
it doesn't go away. it never really goes
away. you just learn to adapt with the pain.

even though you're gone
all of you,
i still keep your name and numbers in my
phone
maybe as a reminder
or maybe hoping to call you again one day.

#voicemail

my facebook has
turned into a platform
where i share obituaries and funeral
locations.

#updatestatus

i wish you would've kissed me in the rain
when i asked.

maybe we'll meet again in a different life,
and things would be different.

even after a long day at work
when i see you everything is familiar,
everything is fine again
and i feel at home.

Spoken word I hope

i feel like i've been here before
but i feel different this time
different time to differentiate the difference
different interests
expecting similar deliverance
i need someone to interfere
my own thought process
cause my process is processing
trolling myself i can't stop commenting
insecurities securing themselves
imbedding into my nerves
forming new paths for my curves
i mean my words

i'm polynesian so i know how to sway but
you can't sway my thoughts
only i can do that
you can't take what i've lost
only God can do that
i'm spiritual but i'm not 'spiritual'

i smoke weed on saturday
to feel higher on sunday
cause some day
that's where i wanna be
floating in the sky
while my body's in the ground
Mother Earth can hold me
because i don't have a mum right now i've
lost 3 of them, important women in my life
took myself out of the night life
so i can see clear
sober from alcohol almost 8 years
that was my choice to make
and if i could go back and do it again, that
would be my curse to break

time traveling to now
to see what's at stake
while the stake goes right through my heart
that had to re-break
loss is a heavy thing
i know i talk about it a lot

but loss is what i bring,
it's what i know
but i'm also here to say
it's how you grow
it's what you show
the seeds you plant in the dirt
is what will glow

so while my mind is a mess
i know i'm planted in something strong
my roots are immovable
and the comments i make about myself are
removable i say this as i'm pushing back my
cuticles maybe i'm nervous
or maybe i don't believe it yet
my thoughts are out of service
while i smile on the surface
drowning while alive
.. i've seen it.
i watched my mum drown
while fluids filled her lungs
making eye contact knowing

the unknowing awaits
while we wait
and wait.

she looked past us,
up to the right hand corner of the room
i wanna see what she saw
i wanted to leave that room too

then she left.

and we were left with what's left
an evicted body with no home
no lights
not sure where to go
felt the pain in my chest,
down to my feet
and the pain was released with every word i
speak i mean spoke
i mean, hope.
i've been looking for hope
i know she's around

i know she's right there but i can't see her
right now. where is she?
i've been opening my front door to let her in
invite her for coffee

maybe she's more of a tea person,
that's why she hasn't called me

so not long ago
i woke up one morning
the sun was on my face
after a night of mourning
warming me on the inside, deep into my
core covering my storm, that was trying to
outperform, me trying to chip away at my
roots
that i told you, do not move

it was hope.

she came back for me
after i thought she'd left

she brought me a life jacket
and I no longer felt like i was drowning,
to death
the warmth was pouring through my chest
had to take off my vest
and as i looked up to hope,
into the light,

and I saw my mum
she came back for me when I thought I was
done.

a collage of distorted images
flood my mind

focus
focus

squint until the images seem somewhat
clear

focus.
but wipe off that rented smile
unless you're willing to pay extra

deep breaths - inhale
taking in this polluted air
deep breaths - exhale
polluting the air

focus
focus past the blurry images
that are almost impossible to figure out

(sometimes i feel like i am almost impossible
to figure out)

so until then,
i will walk this path
eyes half closed - focused
pulling the pieces apart of every image
to make something of it,
to make something of myself.

you're more than what they think of you.

FENUA

i'm a proud Rotuman woman
woven together by generations
ancestral blood
rooted by family
as we place our hands on the ground
wherever our feet touch
we're reminded of who we are
(i'm reminded of who I am)
as our bloodline fades in the physical
it grows in the spiritual
we're blood, we're one
on this earth
and in the afterlife

don't forget your roots
don't forget what made you, you.

About the Author

Michela Perry is a Polynesian (Rotuman) poet, author, visionary, dreamer and an advocate for healing. She started her writing journey in her hometown Fort McMurray, Alberta, Canada. Writing and poetry helped Michela on her self-discovery wave. Writing about dealing with death, losing important women in her life, love and how harnessing that became her healing power. Her vision continues as she puts out more books, bringing her words to life. As her work gains momentum, she hopes you can find peace between her words and share it with others. Also, hoping you can find a piece of yourself in here, too.

Instagram:
https://www.instagram.com/michelaperry_

www.ingramcontent.com/pod-product-compliance
Lightning Source LLC
Chambersburg PA
CBHW061658120626
46550CB00003B/994